Elizabeth Smart was born in Ottawa, Canada, in 1913. She was educated at private schools in Canada and for a year at King's College, University of London. One day, while browsing in a London bookshop, she chanced upon a slim volume of poetry by George Barker – and fell passionately in love with him through the printed word. Eventually they communicated directly and, as a result of Barker's impecunious circumstances, Elizabeth Smart flew both him and his wife to the United States. Thus began one of the most extraordinary, intense and ultimately tragic love affairs of our time. They never married but Elizabeth bore George Barker four children and their relationship provided the impassioned inspiration for one of the most moving and immediate chronicles of a love affair ever written – *By Grand Central Station I Sat Down and Wept*. Originally published in 1945, this remarkable book is now widely regarded as a classic work of poetic prose.

After the war, Elizabeth Smart supported herself and her family with journalism and advertising work. In 1963 she became literary and associate editor of *Queen* magazine but later dropped out of the literary scene to live quietly in a remote part of Suffolk. She died in 1986.

By the same author

By Grand Central Station I Sat Down and Wept
The Assumption of the Rogues and Rascals
A Bonus
In the Meantime
Necessary Secrets

The Collected Poems of

ELIZABETH SMART

Paladin

An Imprint of HarperCollins*Publishers*

Paladin
An Imprint of HarperCollins*Publishers*
77–85 Fulham Palace Road,
Hammersmith, London W6 8JB

A Paladin Paperback Original 1992
9 8 7 6 5 4 3 2 1

A catalogue record for this book
is available from the British Library

ISBN 0 586 08955 1

Set in Perpetua

Printed in Great Britain by
HarperCollinsManufacturing Glasgow

CONTENTS

II A Bonus

INTRODUCTION

In undertaking to write an introduction to the poetry of Elizabeth Smart, I took it for granted that readers of this *Collected Poems* would be familiar with *By Grand Central Station I Sat Down and Wept*. Truly a once-read-never-forgotten book, it was first issued in 1945 by Tambimuttu of Editions Poetry London. I hope, too, readers will be familiar with its less generally appreciated, less intense and dazzling, but more mature sequel of 1978, *The Assumption of the Rogues & Rascals*. Both were republished in 1991 by Paladin simultaneously with the first English edition of Elizabeth's early journals, *Necessary Secrets*.

There are poets whose work can be appreciated by readers who know little or nothing about their lives. I cannot regard Elizabeth Smart as belonging to this category. Her first published work was recognizably autobiographical, and obviously written by someone whose lived experience and relation with language were those of a born poet. Those of us who were lucky enough to meet Elizabeth not long after her arrival in England in the middle of the Second World War were quite unaware of the fact that she had been writing all her previous life.

The early years of my acquaintance with Elizabeth soon became a lasting friendship, which I came to value increasingly the longer I knew her. Over the years I seldom heard her refer to her 'life before George Barker'; never, I think, to her lifelong ambition to become a writer of the kind she most admired; or to her implicit belief in poetry as the most serious form of writing.

Looking back, my most vivid memory is of a beautiful young woman who reminded me of a far more intelligent kind of Veronica Lake – an evanescent screen star whose appeal was at that time at its zenith. With reference to Elizabeth's poem in which she remembers me reading Baudelaire to her while she sat on the stairs during an air-raid with her babies in her arms, I can now see that I did so without proper realization of the fact that she too had been already familiar with *Les Fleurs du Mal* in the original for about ten years. The scene as I remember it took place in the basement of A.P. Herbert's house in Hammersmith Terrace. He had put it at the disposal of Elizabeth and George, probably at the instigation of Julian Trevelyan, installed in nearby Durham Wharf. I'd forgotten the fire-bombs that night: south-west London saw a lot of them in those days. Soon after this incident, Elizabeth moved with her children to the safety of the country – Moreton-in-the-Marsh in Gloucestershire.

If I attempt to unravel such details here, it is because I find the patchwork weaving together of such remembered facts typical of the narrative method evolved in both her prose works and poems. During the years when Elizabeth lived at Tilty in Essex and later at Westbourne Terrace in Paddington, she was working hard and virtually without interruption at copy-writing and journalism in order not only to support herself and her four children but also to have them well educated. In a series of notes first published in *Autobiographies* (edited by Christina Burridge, William Hoffer/Tanks, Vancouver B.C., 1987), she summed up this time in her life as follows:

Love. Children. Earning a living. Friends. Drinking. Pushed too far to do much. Silent years. Desperate from hating. Desperate anxieties. So many levels. On one, it's a thin deep line straight to the point. On others up and down to deal with distractions.

And in a long, painful piece written in November 1976, Elizabeth discussed with herself the agony and boredom of struggling unavailingly to get something satisfactory written. I extract from it these two brief paragraphs:

Painful dribbles, slow, so slow, pile up into a tiny heap, a tiny load of valuable old rubbish. My pile, a poor thing but mine own.

Even 8½ pages of rubbishy scribbling eases the pressure on my trapped explosive energies.

The year after these words were written, Jay Landesman's Polytantric Press brought out the collection of thirty-nine poems entitled *A Bonus*, described by Jill Neville in her introduction as 'distillations of experience which only someone who has suffered all but forgotten nothing could invoke'.

In the first poem, wryly entitled 'There's Nobody Here But Us Chickens', we are given lists of names which indicate the level of durability towards which Elizabeth constantly aspired: Auden, Byron, Blake, Thomas Traherne, Donne, Eliot, Dylan Thomas, Giacometti, and Braque. And this couplet occurs just before the end of this fifty-three line poem:

(Sorry, Empson and Barker and good Sir John:
I know you're there, but too young and flighty to lean upon.)

From her poems themselves, regarded as it is now possible to do as a whole, it is difficult to say on which poets of the past or present, if any, she thought of herself as most inclined to lean. Her voice, even in the early poems she produced before her arrival in England, is recognizably idiosyncratic and her own. Even the discovery in the late thirties of the poetry of George Barker seems to have had no easily discernible influence on her style or use of language, except perhaps in such a poem as 'Song: The Singing Summer Streets'. The writer with whom to my mind Elizabeth Smart had the most striking affinity, though it seems most unlikely she was ever influenced by her, is Anna Wickham (1884–1947). While their lives and backgrounds were wholly dissimilar, their fervent independence and uncompromising honesty and sincerity make them appear kindred spirits. It is not surprising that the themes they most often tackled were basically the same: sexual union and disunion, partnership, motherhood, dissatisfaction, and the constant struggle to fulfil their intrinsic gifts. The first stanza of Anna Wickham's poem 'Self Analysis', first published in 1915, demonstrates the affiliation that can be seen to link two women poets of different generations:

The tumult of my fretted mind
Gives me expression of a kind;
But it is faulty, harsh, not plain –
My work has the incompetence of pain.

The common denominator apparent in this declaration and in certain poems of Elizabeth's, such as 'A Terrible Whiteness' and 'Rhyme Is Wrong', is certainly not incompetence, though the pain is evidently shared.

In his introduction to Anna Wickham's writings (Virago, 1984), R.D. Smith observed: 'From time to time Anna has a quirky, cheeky, wry truthfulness that recalls Stevie Smith.' This reminds me of a stanza in a poem in the present collection called 'The Muse: His & Hers':

Stevie, the Emilys,
Mrs Woolf
By-passed the womb
And kept the Self.

The poem is one of a group of eleven (*Eleven Poems*, Owen Kirton, Bracknell, 1982). Several of them confront the dilemma of a woman writer in her late sixties attempting to find articulation in verse of the obsessions she has had to postpone writing about when younger because her creative energy had had to be expended on domestic cares. Its main argument is that childless women writers are able to be far more freely prolific than exhausted mothers. I have quoted from it because it takes me back, through association, to the summer of 1957, when Elizabeth allowed me to stay several weeks in her flat in Westbourne Terrace in Paddington.

We spent a memorable day in the company of Stevie Smith, at the invitation of the painter Patrick Swift and his wife Oonagh, who occupied a studio-flat somewhere in the country not far to the north of London. After the meal, we all went out into the fields to hunt for mushrooms: a fairy ring, boleti, button mushrooms, and even the rare and startling *Phallus impudicus* hiding under a bush. Later, after a visit to Michael Andrews painting in a nearby studio, we ate the mushrooms for supper. Some tasted revolting, but none made us ill. Elizabeth and I accompanied Stevie Smith in the train back to Palmers Green, where we walked up the hill to the house she had lived in for sixty years. She had been amusing, sometimes caustic, but always agreeable. The fact that Elizabeth was at the time shackled to *Queen* and *House & Garden* provided a bond of sympathy between her and Stevie, who had spent so many earlier years of her life working for Newnes. As we left her door, I might have reflected that her loneliness was also her luck, as it allowed her to devote most of her time to producing her poetry.

During my stay, Elizabeth and I talked incessantly, both cold sober and after a few (and quite often many) drinks. We made almost daily excursions into Soho, usually visiting Muriel Belcher's Colony Room Club, where I would spend the afternoon waiting for her to return from the office where she made decisions or produced or deposited her copy. At this resort, one usually saw Dan Farson, Jeffrey Bernard, John Deakin, David Archer, or caught occasional glimpses of Francis Bacon. Though Elizabeth could seem the personification of candour, I now realize to what an extent this appearance was deceptive. A preoccupation with her mother seems to have haunted her until the end of her life, though it was not something she was ever likely to talk about. It was part of a nucleus of preoccupations that can be seen to have had a determining influence on all her later writings. It surprises me, too, that she so seldom discussed music with me, though she must have known it was something I particularly loved. I had no idea that when she was nineteen she had studied in London to become a concert pianist. I would never have imagined, for instance, her playing Scarlatti, which she had once done very well. Then there was the surrealist couple, Wolfgang and Alice Paalen, who sent me their periodical *Dyn* from Mexico throughout the War, and the rogue painter Varda, all of whom I had met before 1937 through my friend Roland Penrose, but whom I never guessed Elizabeth had once known even better than I. And it was not until recently that I became aware of the role in bringing Elizabeth and George Barker together that had been played by Lawrence Durrell, whom I began to know well in the late 1930s.

A final incident that I recall with pleasure was a dinner-party at Mary Hutchinson's flat in Hyde Park Square. The other guests that evening included T.S. Eliot and his wife Valerie, to whom then he had not long been married. Mary Hutchinson had just agreed to finance David Wright's *X* magazine and had organized a fund in aid of David Archer. She had been close to the Bloomsbury circle and had known Eliot since her youth. Elizabeth had a sincere if characteristically uneffusive veneration of Eliot (as did George Barker, whose publisher and mentor Eliot had been for many years). This opportunity of meeting him in private in the happy golden autumn of his life was a privilege we both appreciated. Eliot was mellower and more benign than I had known him during previous brief encounters: in a word, he was typically uncondescendingly gracious.

It was Stephen Spender who, well over fifty years ago, first drew my attention to the distinction to be drawn between Eros and Agape. Almost all Elizabeth's poetry is inspired by one or the other, often by her own peculiar combination of both. An unusually alert libido and experience of physical and emotional passion are predominantly the source of many of her most characteristic early utterances. In later years this gradually became modulated into the expression of maternal love, love and affection for friends, and, from her childhood on but particularly at the end of her life, the love of 'nature', that is to say (she had no love of abstractions) love of flowers and plants, insects and birds. Her capacity for friendship and loyalty was perhaps the outstanding feature of her character. Compare the vulnerable, unhesitatingly generous sincerity evident in the poems dedicated to such characters as Jeffrey Bernard and Jeremy Reed.

To anyone aware of the circumstances of the death of her youngest child, Rose, the poem with which she commemorated this tragedy must be the most harrowing in this collection. It meant a lot to her to have been able to write it. Only great emotional courage and determination could have enabled her to find any words at all to express the grief which this event caused her.

In January 1934, Elizabeth was already writing in her journal about her 'will to work, and vows, and plans for writing, in a vivid conglomeration. Writing and eagerness to begin at once ... It comes down over me with an awful swoop ... the desire to accomplish something written ... and remorse at beginning twenty and having done nothing.' What is extraordinary is to find her still writing in early 1979:

'I find myself repeating things I said 40 years ago, coming upon them huffing and puffing laboriously, again, again, finding them — but they were never lost.

'If I could only show — *explain*; what? The good, the glory, the splendour, the greatness, the beauty, the beneficence.'

('Diary of a Blockage', *In The Meantime*,
Deneau, Ottawa, 1984)

What was extraordinary about Elizabeth was the insatiable intensity of her spirit, which nevertheless made her so stimulating and such fun to be with; and her lifelong unyielding will to put this spirit's trials and adventures into words. We are still discovering how extraordinary it is that she so often succeeded.

David Gascoyne
Isle of Wight, 7.V.91.

I

Poems 1938—48

TIME LEAPS! TIME BOUNDS!

What kangaroo bounds does time
Take through my planned garden.
Will the lilies survive
Or is chaos the stuff they feed on?
Or sent as a warning only
Saying, praise Him?

Who conducts this raucous symphony
Orders its pace?
The wild crescendo
Beating the heart out of place?
Who hushes suddenly the wind
Or stretches the hours of despair
Makes a rich substance
Or a poisonous gas out of air?

Time leaps! Time bounds!
The impact rocks earth's edges!
Or time lies crouched
Hiding in brambled hedges.
The dust rises
The gardener stands in dismay
The serene dream undone
The light going from the day.

THE FATUOUS FROGS

Shut up! you fatuous frogs,
You duped nightingales trilling in the wood!
All's a mistake, you fall for a stale joke;
Cease your inane, your gullible cheerfulness.

Who will reward you? Who will give you peace?
The hunters with snares have honeyed your fool's-trap day
Puffing their hairy chests with barbarous pride
They gloat, they gloat, while your praise babbles forth.

The night grows dark. Soon you will be afraid.
The net will fall. Stifle your tactless joy.
Before the song is finished the hunters will rise
To eat frogs' legs and feast on nightingales' tongues.

TO BE OR NOT

Who worth keeping survives
Among these seven million lives?
Cluttering New York in droves?

The swallow that wins is beautiful
But here you never can tell.
The winners are proof against hell

And heaven. But tonic will not revive them
And never will they find home
They will be an easy catch for time.

And I? Though memory-prompted complain of the street
Whose slap all footfalls meet
As if it were a mutual combat.

And no eye either welcomes me
Except the leering and tawdry,
Curiosity or envy.

So either I die or retire too far within
Clothe my one good in fatal sin
Whose wall is invulnerable against the ablest engine.

So die, I say, as if choosing a hat
No melodrama but only that
And the water under the bridge is sweet.

Sweet and early and perpetual
And memory in its shimmering face looks well
And its ending kiss hardly hurts at all.

HOW ELABORATE THE BUILDINGS

How elaborate the buildings, the silt pretendings
Through dazzling images of distraction and then finding
A kiss at the ending.

Only O only. A long face drugs my eyes
Dropping Not Welcome signs, Signs of the Times, as he says.
It's a too too terrible world these days.

Terrible. But I swim like a swan not much caring.
Take away the trappings and give truth an airing.
My love my love when will you be here?

LOVE POEM

You are buried in my pillow of fever
And burn heavily in my eyeballs. Your odour
Pervades my bed, and will not be laid.

Though you offer me an orphan future
Which I leave untouched on an unknown doorstep
Medicine is the touch of your lip.

If you called as you do call from the bottom of the sea
I would hear you in my grave easily
I would step down to join you happily.

Brushing the lies aside I shall leave my bed
I shall find you under the Rumanian dead
Under the wreck, still arched for attack.

WHAT SERENE LAND

What serene land is offered to my eye
But I would straddle it with your thigh
Arched for attack? And though too deep
That thrust for me to live can I cry stop
When the wound it bleeds is my only hope?

Winter shelters spring for action
Perhaps you are an unknown gardener
Watering seeds you plant in plotted days
Where there are no focals but your eyes.

Hope and Europe die behind your head.
But I still holding you hold a world
Ripe with unwritten history, to be beguiled
And even now big with child.

BY THE GAS JET

Here I sit who am no wizard
Courting hazard
By the gas jets to keep my eyelashes dry.

And I say cold womb be vocative
Guide the blind.
But no message reaches the hibernating I,

Drowsy as a bear. Nor will it hear
What even dreams forbear
To ignore: Four corpses in the snow. How long
Have they been there? I asked. Four months.
See their stiff mouths.
Are they angels? Were they done wrong?

Their lips are wet with dew sticky as stamen
It is an omen
Shall my child rise out of this cave of snow?

It is the eery tides bring such debris
From hidden seas
Not blood, what is this poisonous flow?

Not blood not tears not semen,
Doomed women,
It is the riddle that will rid you and breed you.

I am riddled with bullets but my will is unwritten
Ceremony forgotten
It is the need freezes me. The need the need.

EXPEDIENCY

The intensity of the wish
Was it a sharp protection against too many looks
Disintegration from violation because the mob saw?

On my mountain a house is
With a yellow door and The Pulley written for cheer
At the climb's end. But it is all ended, the house is sold.

To whom? Who but the acquisitive eyes
Who hate the unmean the successful the careless look
And said 'While you listen to the birds I make the hay.'

Expediency now eats blueberries on my hill
The damned are sipping tea with gossip in the tabernacle's heart.
What sanctuary to you remains undesecrated?

The Collected Poems of Elizabeth Smart

POEM ADVISING ACTION

With graceful strategy the circling hawk
Whips my circling sorrow to dive and strike;
Indiscrete for action the poison oak
Thrusts up her flushed face into attack;
Lizards and herbs and flowers admonish me,
Strict in their innocence: I am cowardly.
Nor will the mourning-dove condone my fault
Who breasts all hazard for a humble scrap
And when she coos courts punishment. My guilt
Is obvious, and I cannot escape.

ESCAPING WORDS

Words, my horses, roam unbroken
In my head, or, tethered,
Wait their wandering master's ride.

They eat grass. They graze.
Or grow fat, but will never win the race
Nor be mythology's beasts;

Adoring with stampedes
The cats and hay rioting with the day
Necessity supplies them on the haphazard wind.

Their manes are braided with care
And, silver-shod, their gallop
Resounds like triumph drums,

Or incites armies and insurrection. But never
Brings them to me to be
Ever and forever carried into the home of my poem.

IMMINENCE OF WAR

By the shores of Lake Superior the castles of grain
Stand in a wilderness no one has measured
But many a wild woman has held upon her mind
Wider and wilder spaces before she went mad.

By the shores of the Ottawa walk exiled queens
Soothed by the snowflake, companioned by the squirrel
And by the blue Gatineau ambassador and moose
Meet in a common misery and start at the sound of a gun.

BUT THE TRAINS SCREAM
AND THE SNOW FALLS

But the trains scream and the snow falls
Like blood into the womb in every weather
But also flaking with forgetfulness the tomb
Feeding and deceiving like the mother of death.

And love that could move mountains droops in the federal prison
For being unregistered. Who will be at hand
To rock the great green cradle in the day
The Indians fathered but will never see?

And O who shall again sail up that Gulf
That welcomed once so royally? The tom-tom
Drummed its own doom. My dispossessed,
My orphan land, who shall inhabit you again?

NO ICE AGE DEODORIZES LOVE

No Ice Age deodorizes love
Its odour outlasts
White frigid winds, it is ousted
By no gas-mask war can prove.

In bed of fever it spirals in the pillow
When hopes of peace die
It emerges from calamity
Moving like spring in the willow.

You whom the snowflake buries
In a Canadian desert, remember
Love's limbs aren't locked by winter's fury
They unfold even in Hull. Love springs from your lip
Where I meet you at the end of the world.

It is bold, writes Welcome on the poverty-stricken doorstep
And over all grasses spreads its smell
Pervasive with tomorrow
Smearing corpses with seeds of daffodil.

LOVE IN WARTIME

When the incendiaries lit the sky
A face smiled its divine calligraphy:
It was Helen crowned with Troy's debris.

Her unmatchable mouth in the roof
Of blood moved in speech like the home of love,
Hanging its moon of reproof:

'My kiss blots history out.
My landslide legend has forgotten
A thousand thousand bones rotting;

'Under the guilty sea
The ships lie; but accuracy
Has been seduced by me.'

Her smile sailed indiscriminately
Among the squadrons of death majestically
And was reflected on the sea.

'The armless Venus carried Pompei's tears
Better than the raided years
Or the cold dances of chameleon stars.'

Then faded. But the rain,
Like lovers' seeds that fall in vain,
Warned me of my sin.

14th STREET AND THE
NEXT GENERATION

The wanting eyes for whom the hamburger is the prize
Rise on the tides who abuse one another with ruse
(O my savage) what a death's head necklace
For the day of doom!

Like claws cruel for the cause
The triumphing tragedy the horror of the time
So lost (O my breast so armoured against invasion)
Dirges in the hour of surge.

One face a desert beacons for a plane
Then drones uncertainly but never descends
And though they burn and blaze her end
Fizzles in the fireproof Mohave.
O it is an end of end.

Entirely over me. (O my broken angel
Bowered in bowels of blood) to atone in tunnels
Praying as you burrow my sun to a son
Rising over me one small clover patch in a likely spot.

THE ESCORT

Plato is waiting, Lady, while you comb your hair
He is batting his golden sandal on the stair
His brow is barred; he is vexed,
He will not kneel down and pray for the frustrated and
    oversexed.

Freud will, Lady, but you do not care
To be seen in heaven with an escort, bare,
Who will lead you rudely up to the king
And say Wait! I can explain everything!

Shakespeare is poor, Lady, and he is not chaste,
His human jacket is shrunken at the waist,
If you go with him you enter by the stage door,
And some of the apostles may think you are a whore.

Jesus will forgive you, Lady, if you arrive at all,
But Mary Magdalene will blackball
You, and O dear Lady, she has more pull
With the Lord now at each fall.

Who dear Lady, O who will wait for you
Or hold your place in the essential queue?
Already all the best places are taken by Jews:
Hurry up, Lady, hurry up and choose.

AS NEAR AS THE CENTRE
OF THE WORLD

As near as the centre of the world lies my bird
Whispering all mysteries. I hear him drop
With chastening silence out of the shricking air
The icicle nightmares at the window appear
But cannot dissolve the magic. All that we feared is here,
Can threaten no longer with the calendar.
Complacent as the earth whose cosmetics are blood
And in the crater nests the new brood
He knocks at the door of the world.
The dead rise to admit him and unborn advocates
Plead his arrival. Angels and fiends wait
For him to signal: All's well with fate.

With what out-distance lens his unborn eyes see
With precipitate passion why he should be
And with his kisses of argument seduces, silences me.

TIME HAS NO SIGNAL FOR ITS WAITING FERRIS WHEEL

Time has no signal for its waiting ferris wheel
Becalmed. And will no water form?
Hardly the silver effusion of moisture from the ceiling
And thousands of trusting waiting with rusting cups.

Below in the parching mud Aphrodite waits
Her listening ear shrivelling as crackles split up her hope,
'My arms! My lovely arms entombed!' No sea to weep
Who will unlock love for the waterless world?

It is a long pause, an endless intermission,
Missing sweet peace. The people turn to begetting,
Wantonly shoving forward into other forms
The wheel's why, the engine's unknown guts.

It was a Fair, at first, and the ferris wheel
Its dazzling view to dare till time's wheel stopped and stuck,
Struck in its flightiest moment to stone the gaudy wing
Sucked to the sun the reservoirs of love.

THE HAGGARD EYES THAT
PROWL THE FUTURE

The haggard eyes that prowl the future
Refuse the gilding sleep
My keeper wrestles with sorrow
Horror and love, and I sit on the parapet.

In simple water it lies too easy under the bridge,
My Faustian pledge with death,
But turns no face of regret
Because five million limp on to a future I refuse.

No, but what, you sentencing hand,
If it has cried in error,
Will never be echoed in water,
And the Chaudiere not turn back and murmur: The moment
　impelled?

POLITICAL POEM

I understand that Christ and Engels kiss,
Engineering a bridge over time, a parasol of shade
For the sheep whom one with a heart and one with a map
Found memorable. Their tears keep flowers wet
To comfort pacifists and the kindly old,
And show there is remedy in recipe and design —
Survivors' herbs, mocked by the ones who died.
But the wound the wound mocks louder and the germ's why
Rises to encourage the cradle to become the tomb
And spare the lean year's rocking and the angry wails
That reach those two who break with solicitude,
Where they peer downward with eyeballs bleeding wisdom,
To bullet the bridge like a wounded bird flapping
'So what? So what?' to their lucid tenderness.

BIRTH OF A CHILD
IN WARTIME

Slapdash into the bloody pan
Is thrown the longed-for son of man.
Between the gossiping cups of tea
God attains mortality.

In the cathedral calm and cold
Kneel the erroneous-memoried old.
But in the womb's cathedral calm
The walls collapse in a birth psalm.

The blood sings from the soiled hand
The apprentice cleans at the washstand
Undismayed by omission,
For everything, everything is won.

The proof blazes in impudence
Above the miopics of science,
Swaggering in love inviolate
Over the uninitiate.

And over all the angels dart
Like squadrons in a war apart
Dropping parachutes of bliss
On everything that is.

SONG: THE SINGING
SUMMER STREETS

Nothing dies, it bursts to birth
Before the requiem is half done,
Before the suitable tears are shed
Or the mourning of the underbred
Nags out its course, the death is dead.

The sighs shoot into the loud trombone
It blows so hard it shakes the earth.
The flowers in a breathless rush break through;
If one has collapsed, then out spring two,
Insatiable for things to do.

It is unnecessary to atone
For sin: he is the losing one;
With all his conjuror's cheap disguise
No geese fly north because of his lies,
No cause is lost, and nothing dies.

I'D RATHER MARRY
A YOUNG MAN

The embryo in the elderly man
Cries out to the dry mammalian gland
But only a devil in the bed
Satisfies a woman's need
Only archangels understand
The less as well as more than human.

O needs that pity urges toward!
O pity urged to kill the need
Of self-survival! Mothering like a map
Beneath wherever you walk is spread
All lovers sporting in her lap
Unable to gambol past the embryonic cord.

My heart and the earth and the stars and the sun
Lurch out of their course an anguished inch
To hear their senile infant cries
A man must suckle before he dies,
Be persuaded, before the avalanche,
That what he has *not* done is not sin.

But oh but oh these comfortable lies
Blare out their falsehood in the gales
When the earth and the stars and my heart and the sun
Revolve because of what they have done
And leave in their dizzy course such trails
Of glory as planets and daisies.

II

A Bonus

THERE'S NOBODY HERE
BUT US CHICKENS

When the elders die
Particularly rather strict ones
Like Auden,
There you suddenly are,
The unstrict inadequate
Old but not wise
Remainder,
Now foolish top dog,
Foolishly left
In the last musical chair.

The words, the works
Were always there.
But they change, or seem to,
When their makers are gone.
No nearer now
(No farther, either)
Than Byron or Blake or Thomas Traherne or Donne.

The metamorphosis starts
The chemical change
(Eliot, Dylan Thomas, Giacometti and Braque)
Cast up, cast down,
Settled, then disinterred,
Forward and back.
Reputations, by people with nothing to do,
Are footballs kicked down the years.
But the goals are never true.

That's one thing
(A slight diversion)
What I meant to say was this:
What about poor old us?
Nudging sixty or seventy or even more
Still hoping that Daddy will pick us up from the floor
And say Tut! Tut! There There
You should try to do better
Should certainly take more care.

Raise your groggy head from this rough dilemma in
Which you find yourself, though you are only feminine
And know if it's going to go on it's got to be you
(And a friend or colleague or two):
Nobody left alive can teach you or reprimand
(Drinking or winking or lending a helping hand
Is not what I mean), it's the empty air beyond
The headmaster's empty study. In fact the entire school's
Empty of masters, *you'll* have to make the rules.
Me? I'm only a learner, one of the fools,
Let me be caretaker, let the children take over.
You can't. You're alive. There isn't any cover.
Shoddy and shy and very unfit for power
They've died and made you an elder in this cold and unjust hour.

(Sorry, Empson and Barker and good Sir John:
I know you're there, but too young and flighty to lean upon.)

So their death isn't the sorrow I thought it would be, the
    passion and pain,
More the bewilderment of a child left out in the rain.

DOUBT IN A GARDEN

Scratch scratch
Clear a patch
Leave it a minute
The weeds are in it.

Why do this
When all that is
Is exquisite
And requisite?

Impose a pattern
On a slattern.
Make a shape.
Commit rape.

It's me O Lord
And I am bored.
I can't stand
The unplanned.

A tree falls
A tree rises
Death appals
Change surprises.

Is it right to change
Thistle for lily?
Rich and strange?
Or just silly?

OUCH! SAYS THE SAINT

Ouch! says the saint as he
Divests himself of the love
Of created objects.
Love! says the hippie
Chickadee dee dee dee!
But when he is bare
And shivering there
What then? says the hen.
How now? my brown cow.
What is this?
Says the instructress.
A cool snowlocked
Wisdom
Out of ear-shot
Scream and kiss.
Calm? Dead?
A better compost
Than most?

BULBS, CORMS, AND TUBERS

It's terrifying in spring
Observing
The unabashed egotistical
Ruthless energy
With which the bulbs thrust free.
It reminds me of the time during the war
When I felt the breath of a bomb just miss me
And careless and colossal
Destroy the house next door.
And though I seem much stronger than any eranthis
Or fragile daffodil, and I have felt force
Or fire or passion, perhaps something worse,
Drive me blindly on,
Yet nothing nothing at all
To compare with a cyclamen.

Plants are millions and millions of years older than us
But they never practise self-abuse.
They don't commit suicide, though they sometimes despair
And decide that the life before them is unfair
And let themselves die. And they can have moods.
But these are mostly alien plants from other latitudes,
Bewildered, and with rhythm all askew
Like aeroplane travellers losing whole days in the blue
Never to be recaptured. Plants in their native lands
Have a thousand tricks and dodges to withstand
Enemies and accidents and they have the humility
To let this earth-shaking energy pass through free;
They never tell lies or pretend

They haven't met with a setback when they have. They bend
Twist, turn, hurry on propagation,
Seeding must be seen to, they're mad about creation.

If it can't be done with happy open petals in the sun
It will be done with smaller less happy ones but it will be
done.
They'll see to it that the bee finds them, the bug and the
butterfly,
And then with a sigh of contentment they'll be content to die
And let the next rampant livers come on and perform:
Enormous grasses, thistles, even, devious bindweed. Then
   bulb and corm
Or tuber goes into a long modest unegotistical rest
Gets baked, soaked, frozen, and doesn't care in the least.
It sits quietly through months in this retreat.
Then suddenly! suddenly! the message comes! Then!
Then! They can burst through concrete!

THE RHYTHM AND
THE RHYME

The rhythm and the rhyme
If the concentration is absolute
They obey the thought
With a little help afterwards.
But for wobbly concentration
The puzzle forms the strictness
Acts like iron lungs
Props to start up breathing.
One a mad pursuit.
One a sly strategy.

A BONUS

That day that I finished
A small piece
For an obscure magazine
I popped it in the box

And such a starry elation
Came over me
That I got whistled at in the street
For the first time in a long time.

I was dirty and roughly dressed
And had circles under my eyes
And far far from flirtation
But so full of completion
Of a deed duly done
An act of consummation
That the freedom and force it engendered
Shone and spun
Out of my old raincoat.

It must have looked like love
Or a fabulous free holiday
To the young men sauntering
Down Berwick Street.
I still think this is most mysterious
For while I was writing it
It was gritty it felt like self-abuse

Constipation, desperately unsocial.
But done done done
Everything in the world
Flowed back
Like a huge bonus.

TRYING TO WRITE

Why am I so frightened
To say I'm me
And publicly acknowledge
My small mastery?
Waiting for sixty years
Till the people take out the horses
And draw me to the theatre
With triumphant voices?
I know this won't happen
Until it's too late
And the deed done (or not done)
So I prevaricate,
Egging them on and keeping
Roads open (just in case)
Go on! Go on and do it
In my place!
Giving love to get it
('The only way to behave).
But hated and naked
Could I stand up and say
Fuck off! or, Be my slave!
To be in a very unfeminine
Very unloving state
Is the desperate need
Of anyone trying to write.

BABIES

Granny told me
About her nine
Children
Emotional mist in her eyes.

But if she went into Barnardo's
And they were each in a cot
(By magic – they're grown-up now)
Would she know which ones she'd got?

Growing is the strange death
In life that nobody mourns
The forgotten babies that filled the whole world
When they were first born.

The Collected Poems of Elizabeth Smart

INSIDE THE BEARDED MAN

Inside the bearded man
The crying baby lies
The disarming face is gone
The flowery flesh is worn
And nobody wants to rush in
To his peevish petulant cries
And wipe his bottom or eyes.

He's in a pitiful mess
But the middle-aged man
No matter how hard he tries
Cannot command the love
That came free with his innocence.
He bawls in vain in his pain
Such comfort will never never come again.

I WANT TO LEAVE A MESSAGE

Are you there?
No, you're not in.
Then I'd like to leave a message:
For if and when we meet
I might be lighting the fires
Or cooking a mess of potage
Or making a dozen beds.
The moment is seldom right
And from action and omission
Which I thought would be full of clues
It's a lot to expect
That others would guess my news.
To me it seemed loud and clear
But it could corroborate error
To you, if you didn't choose
Decoding, wartime, terror.

IN MY SHATTERED GARDEN

In my shattered garden
I lie and cry.
Why?
I could scrub floors
And get a sense
Of something done
A neat
Achievement
But
I get up
And stumble on
And get slapped back.
I count my blessings
Many, many.
It is no use.
Back and forth
I pace
Carrying a deep despair
Like a fretful child.
There there, despair,
There there.

IS THIS PAIN JUSTIFIED?

Is this pain justified?
Set like a monstrous stillbirth
In a Christmas panic —
An unwrappable
Un-depth-chargeable
Gloom.
If memory worked
More than a three-day week
Euphoria would step in
And be my sparkling guest
But I can't recall my loves
And all the old toast-warm
Encouragements.
Courage is the word
But it takes all I have
To carry faith
Like an undernourished twin
To overfed despair.

Only a few hours more
And people and bustle
Will dispel this state.
Flat facts. I know. But know? Truly? No.
I won't reveal this sin
Of unjustified suffering,
Four days of wallowing
In an obscene affair
With a bully who takes advantage
Of me when no-one is there.

How I used to long
For silence and solitude.
Because in a day or two
Out of the blue
Angels descended then
Connecting me with heaven
In a constant consummation,
Independent of men
And things and events
All day and night
A long long amen.

Now they've flown
As is their wont.
Why should they return?
How can I expect
Their brilliant rescue work?
I don't. I feel they've quit
And quite rightly
Why should they flirt
With a psyche so unsightly
Connecting wires pulled out
And electric knowledge gone?

Rooks reel
In a barren field
Heifers munch
Little birds crouch
In a cold bush

The clock ticks
The walls groan
Every tree
Signals futility.

Parcels Christmas-wrapped
Are full of trash.
Weak spirit and weaker flesh
From every sight
The message comes in a flash:
Despair is everywhere.

So what is this pain about?
This unjustified suffering?
Why don't I know
Why I suffer so?
Pacing pacing
The small room
Blind deaf and dumb
Warped by gloom.

IS THERE A MESSAGE FOR ME?

I wanted to leave a message
But now I say
Is there a message for me?
Please see.
Look everywhere
Scour out the cubbyholes
Scoop out the stuff at the back
Search through the notes on the desk
And papers squashed in the grass
Did no-one no-one
Leave a word for me?
Or telephone when I was out?
Or tell somebody something
To tell me when we met?
Not yet?
I can't understand.
Is the post on strike?
The telephone out of order?
I had some friends
And some of them promised to write.
I felt very pampered and rich
It was almost a surfeit.
How could I have then foreseen
This December evening
And my desperate need
For a pulley out of this pit?
If the message should come
Look for me under the ground.

THERE ARE TWO MOVEMENTS
IN A WOMAN'S LIFE

Rock rock
Rub rub
Two movements
Life's nub.
Soothe pain
With a rock.
Make clean
With a rub.
Be rubbed
For love.
Be rocked
For shock.
In a rub
The vigorous hand
From side to side
In aggressive stand.
But real aggression
Comes from above.
Vertical is pain.
Vertical is love.
But horizontal
To keep clean.
Horizontal
To lullaby.
From side to side to still the cry
To ease the ache to dull the pain
From side to side from side to side
Rocking and rubbing the women ride.

CHRISTMAS IS COMING

Under the cracked and cobwebbed walls
Into the cold and dirty rooms
To sit on torn and broken chairs
Christmas is coming.

I'll put on a black cloak covered in hairs
Joss-sticks to camouflage the fumes
And wrap up rubbishy plastic dolls
Christmas is coming.

The many things I need appals
The horror of the undone looms
I haven't even swept the stairs.
Christmas is coming.

Light fires light fires and say your prayers
That the spirit will kill these crouching glooms
And the heart be singing its madrigals.
Christmas is coming.

CLEANLINESS IS *NOT* NEXT TO GODLINESS

Godliness
And cleanliness
Were joined by the devil
To do evil.
Poverty
Can never be
Clean, nor can
Misery.
Snot and tears
Piss and shit
Usually
Accompany it.
Soap costs money
So do baths;
Are for the haves
Not the not-haves.
The minute your house
Is shining clean
Pride rises up
And comes between .
You and God,
And self-esteem
Is your new
Unholy dream.
If clean is pleasant
In your eyes,
Clean, but then
Apologize.

Cleanliness, like lust
Drink, food
Is beautiful
But not of God.

ACCUMULATION

Boredom and guilt
Drive one on
In a slow
Accumulation.

How weak are vanity
Lust and ego.
But it wasn't like this
For Victor Hugo.

Men find power
An ignition
Cast off cares
Of accumulation.

But that's for living
For getting by:
Pleasure! Nature
Is trite and sly.

But seek the pearl
O oyster soul.
The whole the hole
The hole the whole.

Horror and terror
Nightly seen
But in between
Serene! Serene!

They talk right
Now of survival
But trees wait.
Join the right side.

When a word's in the air
It's indication:
Catastrophe reaching
Consummation.

The slow slow play
The turgid novel
The cautious poem
Are infidel.

And useless too
Decades late:
Nothing there
To accumulate,

Just catching a whiff
After the lion
Hunters.
Tatterdemalion!

A TERRIBLE WHITENESS

Every writer
Except flibbertigibbets
Feels the horror
Of the blank page.
Out of a million million permutations
To pull the three or four words
That move into a nucleus —
How can it be done?
Pressing down on the nerves
Like bursitis
Something wants to get out.
Lance in the wrong place
And you do not get release
But aggravation
And loss of concentration.
Envy the bold surgeon
With his sharp knife
Smiling and certain above the white body.

CPS & JBP

'A book should serve as an axe for the frozen sea within us'
Kafka

No frozen seas are locked within
CPS and JBP
They write with pleasure sweet as sin
Not like me oh not like me
I'm anguished to know how to begin
Held in horror like a gin
Every word an agony
Yet not to write a treachery
What would you do JBP
If you were me if you were me?

Why is it easy, CPS?
Where is the boredom? Where the mess?
Just neat white paper covered with words
Or are they turds or are they turds?

Have you a trick to teach me, please,
About releasing the frozen seas?
Have you an axe that's sharper than mine?
Or an understanding with the divine?
A pact with the Muse? A discipline?
Or does it depend on what's within?

Within CPS and JBP
Things must be very orderly.
Everything flows and nothing baulks
They take the Muse for domestic walks
Pile up pages like games of golf
Strenuous maybe but satisfying
(Some people don't even know they're lying)
A tiny triumph every day
That is the way that is the way.

Don't go exploring don't dig deep
Eschew all friendships with the worms
Learn the ropes and nautical terms
And watch the weather for dangerous storms
Then like me you'll never be
Locked in the sea locked in the sea
CPS and JBP.

LITTLE MAGAZINES

Hungry red-wristed
Keepers of the true
Small unsentimental tone
Or thread or litmus paper
That in the midst of madness
Or chaos or revolution
(When passions obscure
And everyone repudiates
What he knew)
Steadily sturdily
Keep a small-sized
Truth in view
(Small-sized is
The embryo too):
Them I salute
Because we can't go out on a limb
Without guardians
Like them.
Eddie Linden, for instance,
Let us hymn.

TO PATRICK KAVANAGH ON READING HIS POEM 'IS'

Paddy Kavanagh
How right you are
In your poem called 'Is'
I find catharsis.
I meant to quote a line
And say Thanks! How you've enriched mine!
But like a good poem it was a whole
Its Wyatt-like deceiving syncopation only a role
To baffle the gullible pompous. They shy from raw soul.
The next thing, the new startler, seems too simple to be good,
Too close, impertinently personal. But they're polite, you're
    rude.
Like sex, babies, plants, animals and private life.
How alive, Kavanagh, how obstreperous you are in your grave,
Waiting, as you advised yourself,
Probably singing out of tune,
For time to pass, and what you did to be known.

Once you said I was all right
And I felt proud then,
But prouder now
When I read this poem and say Amen.

PARENTAL DOUBT

Doubt, parental doubt
Is a heavy sort of thing
To carry about.

Did you realize this
When you became pregnant,
My pretty miss?

That thirty years on
You might have a
Reproachful son,

Begun in love
But now saying 'Mother Mother
What were you thinking of?'

Do you realize, my dear,
Ecstatically knitting booties
That whatever you do you won't be able to please:
Your daughter says, 'Damn you, it's all your fault, my
    neurosis!

'You shouldn't have left me then
I'm all screwed up
I have to be mean to my man.'

Or even, 'You did too well!
Our childhood was one long paradise
Your glittering world turns out to be all lies:
Why didn't you give us a healthy taste of hell?'

Forty years on from there
When you see them puff and slip on the dangerous stair
Trying to get up and on
Will you be too old to care

If they now say, 'Mother Mother
We know what it's all about.
How did you cope with *your* parental doubt?'

What a bitch Dame Nature is,
My pretty miss,
Lucky you procreate in ignorant bliss.

THE USEFUL DEAD

Are alive people any more
Use than the dead are?
Is it better to ring up Hetta
Than open Byron?
Better to make a date to meet for a drink
Than look at the letters of Swift?
The dead cost you no money, effort, tact,
And they can't answer back.
They can't listen. But then
Neither do the living.
Well, hardly ever.
The dead can inspire, fire, seem to sympathize,
And can't hide under their lies
Which lie open, probed by inquisitive scholars
Conscientiously earning American dollars
Or a footnote in history. The marriage is rather blank
In bed with the dead. Is it better than a wank?
Is it fruitful or just instructive to flirt with Proust?
As a real-life friend he must have been one of the worst.
Don't telephone anyone: write it all down.
Maybe someone will understand you better after
    you're gone.

WINTER LANDSCAPE

In the garden rotted bodies are fallen
Black leaves crashed
Asparagus pride decayed
Moss and creeping buttercup taking advantage
Of the mightier out-of-combat.

Still alive, birds hunched against hard times.
Burrowers, moles and mice and subterranean rats
Ravenous, ravage at the roots.

MINING

Little by little a little
But the gold lies low below
Even the best spade in an old hand
I know I know I know
Can't move the rubbish dump
If the faculties are limp.

The trustless tools are sharp
Well-tempered in the harp
But the tune lies low, buried and lost in the sand.
Keep faith. O faith I keep
But the bone can't feel the flesh.
There's an end to congress.

Year after year there falls
The leaves that time expels
Soil is spattered with sifting, silting, rotting.
I know these elementals
But where can the entrance be
To the mine in me?

Little by little a little
But the reckless miner digs
Minerals maddeningly there but perhaps not there.
O for the truffle dogs
To help divine where the helpless treasure's certain
And the last strength put out
On the right route.

HANGOVER

Diabolical Dionysius
Last night egged us on
To raze the sacred temples.
The god has gone.
Now troupes of mini-builders
Using their mini road drills
With puritanical fury
And vindictive zeal
Riot round *my* temples
Needed for enduring
This frail day.

RHYME IS WRONG

Rhyme is wrong
For my irregular heart
It brings in ghostly masters
And sets the mind at puzzles
That's anyhow prone to baulk.
Am I burning the midnight oil
The candle at both ends
Sitting alone and hammering at my sores?
Shall I shut out the night
Faint vertical ash-tree lines?
For somebody watches from the top of the bank,
Never a friend, always inimical,
Why not a guardian angel on the job?
Then it would be all right
Not to shut out the night
And have to be far too closely cocooned with hammer and sores,
Trying out rhyme
Like a band aid on a wound
That needs a surgeon and operating table
To do the least good.
For anyhow rhyme is wrong
For me and my lopsided song
And ghostly masters jeer
And the mind comes all over queer
And won't respond.

MARGERY KEMPE

They fled from the boisterous sobbings of Margery Kempe
With fourteen children, husband and sins behind her
Now in her white and righteous robes
Noisily full of herself and her new vision
That plunged like a thunderbolt into her unread mind
And set her middle-aged legs
On the road to the Holy Land.
She couldn't write, so she had to make a noise.
They complained and avoided her company
(Especially in church
Where she really was outrageous
In the loud expression
Of her new-found passion).
An excessive lady
She tells us herself —
Far too fond of love
Even if the lover was her husband
And he, poor fellow,
Driven to incontinence and premature senility
(Another good reason for changing her direction).
A lovely terrible person
But a bit too much on a long dusty pilgrimage —
Better to travel with her now
When many centuries tone down the din.
A quiet Dutch scholar wrote it all down for her,
Bullied, no doubt, but his careful script never wavered,
And he kept his smiles suppressed
Till the self-revealing tale was told.

ARE FLOWERS WHORES?

Flowers aren't choosy
Which bee which bug
Come one come all.

Bees and bugs
Aren't choosy either
All entries sweetly natural.

Imagine a flower
Closing its throat
Against a bee it thought a bore.

Who said object
Should excite act
That *that* was moral?

If only the verb
The act acts,
Why call your sister a whore?

Sin and shame!
Abandon the word
Moral. You can *see* it's immoral.

THE GREAT BLUE SPRUCE

The great blue spruce
has trouble carrying her babies:
The branches break
in the gusty spring gales
and the toasted tip clusters
nestled in the needles
lie in the dusty road –
a fabulous thrown-away work of art.

THE MALE FRUIT

The male fruit
of the red pine
is not at all
like the round bouncy female:
but small and limp and curled
like a discouraged worm
it lies on the boards of my grey table
abandoned from above
with a few spent needles.

THE ANXIOUS MOTHER SPIDER

The anxious mother spider
with a giant ball of babies
staggers in a spidery way
across a desert of brown chips.
Elsewhere it is a brilliant summer's day
and the blue jays
seem to have no serious troubles.

A LITTLE NEWT

A little newt,
translucent orange,
still, and falsely safe
in the newly-turned sandy orange road,
exquisitely erroneous,
obeys his ancient genes.

I moved his vulnerable body
into the green jungle on the side.
He's saved, for the moment,
though perhaps at the cost of
considerable confusion of mind.

AN ARROGANT SNAIL

An arrogant snail
for purposes of his own
thought fit to cross
the gravelled road
at his own majestic pace.
And even if the cars flashed past
with a speed and fury
far beyond birds of prey,
so that he wouldn't even have time
to withdraw into his frail
shell,
still,
because they were so fast,
and he so slow,
he might have been missed,
and his unwise policy
justified.

BEAVER

Beaver,
I liked that tail-slapping
on the waters of the
tangled pond.
It didn't seem serious,
more like an effete keeping up
of forms;
a salute to old wisdom,
now a bit of a bore,
but done perfunctorily,
just in case.

TWO DOGS

I met two dogs in the wood.
We all stopped dead,
shocked by the unexpected.
Wolves? I thought,
distractedly trying to remember
where I was.
Human? they thought in panic,
rigid with guilt
and their secret purpose
to lay a forbidden deer.
We went our separate ways,
shaken,
without a single sound.

LADIES' TRESSES

Ladies' Tresses
is a lady-like white orchid,
found in New England
in damp sunny meadows,
inconspicuous
and self-effacing, but
immaculately righteous and upright
among the coarser weeds.

THE SHEPHERD'S PURSE

How does the shepherd's purse,
newly germinated,
harried by genealogical messages
urging him on
since the ice age,
suddenly feel
an unfriendly hand near,
dealing death
to all his tall relations,
and decide to change
into a perfect miniature,
so that a quick inconspicuous
propagation can take place?

BLAKE'S SUNFLOWER

1

Why did Blake say
'Sunflower weary of time'?
Every time I see them
they seem to say
Now! with a crash
of cymbals!
Very pleased
and positive
and absolutely delighting
in their own round brightness.

2

Sorry, Blake!
Now I see what you mean.
Storms and frost have battered
their bright delight
and though they are still upright
nothing could say dejection
more than their weary
disillusioned
hanging heads.

III

Eleven Poems

THE MUSE:
HIS & HERS

His pampered Muse
Knew no veto.
Hers lived
In a female ghetto.

When his Muse cried
He replied
Loud and clear
Yes! Yes! I'm waiting here.

Her Muse screamed
But children louder.
Then which strength
Made her prouder?

Neither. Either
Pushed and shoved
With the strength of the loved
And the unloved,

Clashed, rebuked:
All was wrong.
(Can you put opposites
Into a song?)

Kettles boiling!
Cobwebs coiling!
Doorbells ringing!
Needs haranguing!

The Collected Poems of Elizabeth Smart

Her Muse called
In her crowded ear.
She heard but had
Her dirty house to clear.

Guilt drove him *on*.
Guilt held her *down*.
(She hadn't a wife
To lean upon.)

'The dichotomy
Was killing me,'
She said, 'till old age
Came to assuage.'

'Now! Muse, Now!
You can have your way!
(Now . . . what was it
I wanted to say?)'

Used, abused,
And not amused
The mind's gone blank –
Is it life you have to thank?

Stevie, the Emilys,
Mrs Woolf
By-passed the womb
And kept the Self.

But she said, 'Try
And see if it's true
(And without cheating)
My Muse can do.'

Can women do?
Can women make?
When the womb rests
Animus awake?

Pale, it must be,
Starved and thin,
Like hibernating bear,
Too weak to begin

To roar with authority
Poems in the spring
So late in the autumn
Of their suffering.

Those gaps! It's decades
Of lying low;
Earth-quaked, deep-frozen
Mind askew.

Is it too late
At sixty-eight?
O fragile flesh
Reanimate!

Eschew, true woman,
Any late profligacy
Squandered on the loving of people
And other irrelevancy,

Useful in the dark
Inarticulacy,
But drop it like poison now
If you want poetry.

Let the doorbell ring
Let the fire men
Put out the fire
Or light it up again.

Sheepish and shamefaced
At nine A.M.
Till the Muse commands
Her ritual hymn,

See lucky man
Get off his knee,
And hear now his roar
Of authority!

This test-case woman
Could also be
Just in time for
A small cacophony,

The Collected Poems of Elizabeth Smart

A meaningful scream
Between folded womb and grave,
A brief respite
From the enclave.

A WARNING

This old woman
Waddles towards love,
Becomes human,
But the Muse does not approve.

This going flesh
Is loved and is forgiven
By the generous,
But houses a demon,

Hullo, my dear, sit down,
I'll soothe your pain;
I've known what you've known,
But won't again,

Though passion is not gone,
Merely contracted
Into a last-ditch weapon,
A word not dead,

A mine unexploded,
And not safe
To have near the playground
Of innocent life.

Keep clear of this frail
Old harmless person:
Fifty years' fuel
Of aimed frustration

Could shatter the calm
And scald the soul
And love fall like napalm
Over the school.

URGENCY AND ENERGY

Urgency
Brings energy.

And energy
Makes urgency.

From urgency a dying poet speaks.
From energy an adolescent wrecks.

One with a purpose
Heaves old bones,
Risks collapse
For what he knows.

The other, filled
With unholy rage
For holy strength
He cannot gauge,

Hurtles towards hurt,
Destroys his day:
By blind mistake
Iconoclast.

Missions, omissions,
Dangerous needs!
Pray shaping spirit
Supervise their deeds.

BIRD AND ADOLESCENT

How well birds
manage their bodies.
Look how they shake off
the rain,
cheerfully surveying
the prospect
for interesting
things to eat.

Where are they huddled
when they're not
hopping about;
when it's all silent
and the air is empty
of their
flighty forays?

A while ago
they were so
busy and thick
you almost collided
with them
walking across
the lawn.

And now, nothing.
Each in his retreat
waits
in rain-enclosed
silence.

Suffering?
It seems not.
They sit,
in expected acceptance,
wide-eyed
for the next
development.

How could you explain
this to an
adolescent,
throwing himself in despair
into a deck chair?
Hurling his turmoil into the calm air —
if it's clouds for him it's clouds for all
So there!

But after time passes,
perhaps,
and his mind clears,
he sees the birds there,
and round unclouded eyes
stare out
bright rebuke.

PUB POEM 1:
THE MERRYMAKERS

When you've done well
There's nothing to tell.
'Help! Help!' cry the prisoners.
'Don't bore!' say the revellers,
'A pint, a bird, a mighty cockstand!
Defeat is not on our mind.
We replenish our stores,
We've nothing to buy from bores.

'Bones like "Life" we've gnawed all day:
It's time for play.
The best jokes are thrown off along the way.'
See them retreat, the prisoners,
Into an eating silence,
Grey, pent up in the corner.
Catatonic! Impotent!

Mercy, merrymakers!
Not every day is a great making day.

PUB POEM 2:
TREACHEROUS SURFACES

I said: 'All surfaces are treacherous
All depths are well.
Hold my hand while I tell.'

But he was lecherous
And broke the spell.

I see: all art is unnatural.

PUB POEM 3:
EXCHANGE AND MART

Exchange and Mart:
You can't have this
But I'll give you that.
Hullo! Have a pint!
Not praise but a kiss.
You'll have to make do
With what is:
You help me, I'll help you.
A financial swizz!
Sometimes a block of gold
For pins!

But *someone* benefits:
The market spins!

WHAT IS ART? SAID DOUBTING TIM

It's *not* leaving your mark,
Your scratch on the bark,
No, not at all
'Mozart was here' on the ruined wall.
It soars over the park
Leaving legions of young soldiers
Where they fall.

Dido cried, like a million others.
But it isn't her tears
That sear the years,
Or pity for girls with married lovers
That light up the crying I
With the flash that's poetry:
It's the passion one word has for another.

It's shape, art, it's order, Tim,
For the amorphous pain;
And it's a hymn,
And it's something that tears you limb from limb,
Sometimes even a dithyramb;
A leap from gravity,
That feels, in the chaos of space, like sanity.

The maker makes
Something that seems to explain
Fears, delirious sunsets, pain.
What does the rainbow say?
Nothing. But a calming balm comes
From Form — a missile that lasts
At least until tomorrow
Or the next day.

THE SMILE

What does it mean
The smile on the face
Of the embryo?
From nine months' nesting
A comfortable afterglow?
Or a smile of triumph
For getting where a million million others
Failed, but
Wanted to go?

It's not like the smile
On the face of the newly dead.
Though people say peace
Achieved at last,
Face relaxed,
Frowns ironed out.
No triumph there
When we get to where
We have to go
Whether we wanted to or no.

The smile on the face
Of the nearly or
Newly born
Is beatitude, is bliss
Far beyond ignorance,
Or absolute comfort
In a safe cocoon.
What can it mean
That nobody ever enters the world
With a frown?

A MUSICAL NOTE

Sometimes Handel
is loud, triumphant, insistent.
I wanted to say Shut up!
Can anything really be *that*
successful and sure?
It must be a lie
and a noisy one, too.

Then he introduces
a note of soft seduction,
and I am abashed,
and ashamed,
and blush
to the music
of the spheres.

END OF A SUNFLOWER

A pheasant found a sunflower,
And perched on the arch,
And munched,
A little every day at an early hour.

What a way to go —
Obscene remains ragged on the tall stalk,
Startling the tactful dying all around,
The soothing autumn sinking-away-in-a-glow —

A murdered man on show!

IV

New Poems

OLD WOMAN, FLYING

Why shouldn't an old woman fly?
The Duchess of Bedford amazed in aeroplanes.
But it's flights of fancy I'm thinking of, I
Feel fancy still tickling beloved epitomes.

   Old Mr Yeats
   Reached new heights
   Contained his rage
   Against old age
   And caused the best poems to be won
   When he was a very old person.

So much the better if he couldn't get it up.
When energy's oozing you should cherish each drop in a cup
Until enough is gathered for a celebratory draught
To share with contrary Muse. Nothing is, aft

   er all, too late
   If you don't insult or hate her
   (and he never did)
   Why should she not recur?
   He was her friend:
   Was it likely she'd desert him towards the end?

So, pale and pendulous on my shaky bough
I get ready for take-off, jeered by hoi polloi.
But wait! watch! follow with eyes, mind,
(There are so many things far better left behind)
And then like a good bird-watcher you just might
See useful manoeuvring in this late flight,

A hello, a hooray,
A greeting along the way
A well, well, then
So it can be done:
An instigatory vesper
In a setting sun.

ROSE DIED

Unstoppable blossom
above my rotting daughter.
Under the evil healing
bleeding, bleeding.

There was no way to explain
the Godly law: pain.
For your leaping in greeting,
my failure, my betrayal,

shame for my cagey ways,
protective carapace;
blame for my greeting leaping
over your nowhere place.

Spring prods, I respond
to ancient notes that birds sing;
but the smug survivor says this is *after* the suffering,
a heavenly lift, an undeserved reward.

Your irreversible innocence
thought heaven now, and eternal,
was surprised, overwhelmed,
by the painful roughly presented bill,

the hateful ways of the ungenerous.
But, loving the unsuspecting flower,
could love urge bitchiness
as a safe protective covering?

O forgive, forgive, forgive,
as I know you would,
that my urgent live
message to you failed.

Two sins will jostle forever, and humble me
beneath my masked heart:
it was my job to explain the world;
it was my job to get the words right.

I tried, oh I tried, I did try,
I biked through gales,
brought hugs, kisses,
but no explanation for your despair, your desperate Why.

With its smile-protected face,
my survival-bent person
is hurtled on by its nasty lucky genes,
its selfish reason,

and greets the unstoppable blossom
above my rotting daughter,
but forever and ever within
is bleeding, bleeding.

ALICE I

Alice
you must keep open
a place
for things to begin.
Their flying around,
their tapping at an old wound,
show
how urgent they grow
to enter you.

They might come
they may have come
when all was closed,
shut, dark,
cold —
(they die in the cold);
even extravagant seeds
with millions of siblings
spare
cease on the concrete street.

ALICE II

Alas, Alice,
no day's eye
to close in gloom;

curiouser and curiouser
the No's you use:
No's no use for bloom.

Is this a policy, daisy?
Am I being bossy?
Appalled I risk

the pedantic tone, lecture
uselessly, and the mote in my eye
dances sarcastically.

IN THE WHISPERING HELLS

In the whispering
hells of Academe
I pussyfoot around.
Are you anti-doting
at my side,
Virgil? Dante?
as I nose out
places where they file
passion, cross-
referenced
for sometime use

Assail, or sob,
or scream a battle cry?
There she goes mad or drunk
they'll say.
Sad heart,
Indignant mind,
trying to restrain distain
for a better way —
If they should speak?
If I reply?
This hope dies every day.

POOR CAGED CANADIANS

Poor caged Canadians
Drinkless or drunk
the emotions dozing below
or erupting like burst radiators
ruining the car,
breaking the journey,
obscuring the destination:

Stand fast in vastness —
there's enough of it! —
buried in blizzards
if need be,
keeping the sweet
communion that makes a man
fit into his body like a
precious event,
a perfect treasure,
or a germ
hold the beginning
after the scary end.

A BELL

There's a new bell on my door
It will ring as never before.

There's a new fish on my hook
It's giving me an old-fashioned look.

Unconscious says it's good to eat.
Conscious says it looks like dirt.

Wily fishermen must be prepared
For novelties, old boots, even to be ensnared.

The new bell's up. It's ready to ring.
My God! But it's almost evening.

No sound. It must be Early Closing Day.
I thought you said to take the hard way.

Maybe I got confused. Most ways are hard.
(And frozen today.) Could I have not heard?

Don't come. Don't ring. Unless you're the real McCoy
Rushing to open to duds I should certainly not enjoy.

I'll wait (the greater part of wisdom, life
And fishing) the eternal *motif*.

But I'll get my greeting ready and I'll cook my fish
Today might just be the day that I get my wish.

O POOR PEOPLE

Let us invoke a healthy heart-breaking
Towards the horrible world,
Let us say O poor people
How can they help being so absurd,
Misguided, abused, misled?

With unsifted saving graces jostling about
On a mucky medley of needs,
Like love-lit shit;
Year after cyclic year
The unidentified flying god is missed.

Emotions sit in their heads disguised as judges,
Or are twisted to look like mathematical formulas,
And only a scarce and god-given scientist notices
His trembling lip melting the heart of the rat.

Whoever gave us the idea somebody loved us?
Far in our wounded depths faint memories cry,
A vision flickers below subliminally
But immanence looks unbearably; TURN IT OFF! they hiss.

HELLO

Hello Hello
From the depths of the well.
But can you hear me
When I'm so low?

I'm prowling in a cave
Deep underground
So my words might have
An inarticulate muffled sound.

I'm hacking through
Deep frozen matters
And they give off gasses
Not very nice for lads and lasses.

But I see you there
Wrestling with your muses
Trying to light bombs
With burnt-out fuses.

I know you're wooing
The treacherous word
Trussed-up with feelings
And tired of being unheard.

How kind you are
To sit quietly there
Not raising a shout
And giving me the benefit of every doubt.

I feel for your wounds
Your wasted spirits
Your misplaced pride
Your unregarded merits,

I'm loving your loving
Admiring your courage
Even respecting
Your camouflage,

Your necessary mask,
Your hopeless job,
Your giving to Oxfam,
Your singing robe.

So I say Hello
From the depths of the well
And they lie who say
This love is apocryphal.

SLIGHTLY RHYMING VERSES FOR JEFF BERNARD'S 50th BIRTHDAY

My Dear Jeff,
I can't say enough
how much I admire
the way you have
conducted your entire
life, and the way you have
used your marvellous Muse.
And how right she was to
choose you. Because
she's a Rare Bird who would
have retired or died
if you hadn't known how
to amuse
her, and her you.
That's one non-bogus
marriage made
on Parnassus
and *true*.

She knew
exactly what and who
she was letting herself
in for: the real You.
Drink, betting shops and pubs
are the sort of thing that rubs
her up the right way:
she'll always stay
and make you more beautiful
and witty
every day.

This is a loose love
Ode, owed
to one of my friends
who is in my special
collection of people
who make amends
for endless excruciating
boring hours
so often lived
when foolishly pursuing
stimulation,
and none occurs.

Sterne, Benchley, Leacock,
Carroll, and Nash, and Lear
are not more dear
to me than bedrock
Bernard (3).
(Do I not pay 65p.
ungrudgingly weekly,
for a fixative laugh,
uniquely Jeff?,
who has become
a consolatory
addictive to me?)

Wilde would have smiled
and been beguiled
and bright enough to know
that *you* had a better

Muse in tow
than he.
Could he see
the angelic emanations
from gutters where we
all fall, while
trying to pee,
and rise, or try to rise,
unwisely, in majesty?

And Swift is bitter
and cross
and doesn't make us
feel better
at bearing our lot,
and, in his rage
at the odds,
misses the old adage
that recurs to me
often, in every mess:
'against stupidity
even the gods
are helpless.'
He
lifted furious fists
but had no effect
on the jibbering idjits.

Your subject is not mean,
who's up, who's in,
or jockeying for position
(what a dreary sin).
Funny but kind,
your subject is justly seen
as the inexhaustible one
of nude mankind:
Yourself, in fact, drinking,
amidst the alien corn,
and explaining the amazing joke
of being born.

Your sources —
grief and love
and the Coach & Horses
and all the things we're
thinking of
but don't admit,
because they don't fit
our grand ideas of
our own importance.
You hit the
soul on the head
when it rises
out of its lying bed,
pompous with portents
above its station,
and greedy for rewards
above its ration.

But you're never snide,
and you never hurt,
and you wouldn't want to win
on a doctored beast,
and anyhow the least
of your pleasures
resides in paltry measures.

So guard, great joker God, please guard
this great Bernard,
and let 1982
be the most brilliant year he ever knew.
Let him be known
for the prince of men he is,
a master at taking out of
himself and us the piss.

If you will do this, God,
I'll be good all year,
and try to be better-dressed,
and soberer, and keep my prose-style clear,
(for this great man
is embedded in my heart)
I'll remain, Sir, then and only then,
Yours sincerely, Elizabeth Smart.

TO JEREMY REED 1982

Jeremy Reed
I saw your need
But I'm as shy as you are
And more terrified by far
Except with very emotional ways of being
Or dead drunk late in the evening.

I like your verse
Your tortured face
Your black nails give me a frisson
A touching je ne sais quoi
Of panache and bravado.
I had helps like that long ago.

But now I'm old
And not so bold
I get nakeder day by day
So what could I say
That would be useful to you
In this trying period you're going through?

I suppose
No one knows
The suffering, heaving and crying all around
So I just try to make a cheerful sound
Scattering banal love like confetti
Over everybody's funeral and wedding.

You slipped like a ghost
(It was opportunity lost)
Behind a pillar at Tambi's do.
I was waylaid, being irrelevant and brave
Braved for the worst in such a social enclave.
And the wine disagreed
Or I would have searched for you until I found you
And attended to your need.

So, Jeremy, sorry!
But don't worry
Chance may do better sometime, this or next year
And we can exchange a word of good cheer
Or sympathy or stimulation or encouragement.
Anyhow, thank you for the kind words you sent.

TO DAVID GASCOYNE, ON HIS 65th BIRTHDAY, SOME BLUE HIMALAYAN POPPIES, FIRST FOUND ON THE ROOF OF THE WORLD BY AN INTREPID PLANT-HUNTER, AND THESE INADEQUATE VERSES FROM HIS FRIEND ELIZABETH

Count the amount of us left alive
When a young man reaches sixty-five
(I paraphrase a mutual friend
But he won't mind). It's not the end
It's the new beginning I celebrate
A true success story none can emulate
Because there's none so true.
David Gascoyne, Happy Birthday to you!

Many happy returns to him
Who kept the Muse safe under his thumb
Though trapped in troubled silences for years.
Who kept, though tortured, his integrity.
It cheers each lonely soul to know such things can be.
(It certainly does me.)

I remember I was there
When fire-bombs slashed the street
I sat on the stair
Beneath your feet
Two babies in my arms
And you read Baudelaire.

As the flames leapt
And people ran with water
I clutched my daughter
And son, and wept.
You said: 'Le désespoir a des ailes
   L'amour a pour aile nacré
   Le désespoir
   Les sociétés peuvent changer.'
You quoted Jouve.
We did not move
Until it was all quiet
And we found we were not dead.

And I remember how you stood
Uneasily at the window
And you said
'There's something horrible in the paper'
And held out the Evening Standard
With a quiet rage
With sweet friend Margery lying smashed
On the pavement, slashed
Across the front page.

Your educative silences
(Like brackets enclosing
Enormous sympathy
Too huge to speak)
Recur like essences
To strengthen me when I am weak.

Teacher, reaffirmer
Of the good;
Repudiator
Of the stupid;
Kind ignorer
Of the mediocre
(You remain always polite
To the poor human)
Accept my gratitude.

Friend through all my inarticulate years
Consoler of my so inordinate tears
Intrepid bringer of the good news
Elegant sharer of gutters, dilemmas, blues,
One among many I raise my glass to say
October the tenth is a great day
And how lucky for us you decided to come this way.

So let's take up the blue guitar
And tell the world how wonderful you are
It's true it's true it's true
Happy birthday happy birthday happy birthday to you.

ALL I KNOW ABOUT WHY I WRITE

My poor blind passion wells up, though
forced by expediency sometimes to hold its tongue.
Some saw an appalling innocence (naked
naivety). They saw with blush and *frisson*.
It reflected back.
So passion crouched, crouches.
So, squashed, fights feebly back.
It can't *not*.
The message is like the one in the genes.
It *can't* be disobeyed.
(O flagging prizefighter, lurching from bloody corners —
there's game for you!)

To examine this tottering passion?
What, whence, why, whither?
Measure and weigh it?

I think not.

Men and boys delight in diverting caterpillars
from their destination.
They laugh. Why?
It's the dogged orientation that again and again
insists on its original destination.

This poor pre-butterfly I see in me, this caterpillar
passion, balked but cocky, is the pet I must protect, feed,
understand the needs of. (Needs must, when the devil drives.)
   This caterpillar is not masked − how silly can you get? −
he's naked as a drop of water. He has no shell, no pupa, no
   cocoon.
His necessary helps are delicate, subtle, require domestic angels
to cater to his needs. His habits are not heretofore known; and
his destination is blurred.
   I talk in riddles. I'd rather speak plainly.
   But some ways are still unmapped.

   Yes, every morning, when light reflects
in the West (can't see the East), the unsquashable
urge arises, wobbling its unseeing hopeful head
about − is this the day? at last? now?
   It's embarrassing to harbour such a worm;
to go so unclothed among the gossiping of the concrete world:
a slow organic matter moving over the plastic palaces
in a ridiculous search for an unknown destination.
   But this happens, most days of the week.

   Disobedience (what a well-packed portfolio
this word is) to *anybody's* messages from genes
breeds disaster (cancer, for instance, constipation,
coldsores, brain tumours, rhumatoid arthritis) −
the pilot must act when the antennae receive the coded order.
   Or he's a bad boy.
   Not fit for his duties.
   And will be fired from the Force.

(the Forces: there's another strong-armed
word innocently giving away its aims.)

Indefatigable it is, and must be, this poor blind
passion welling up every dawn for seven long decades.
Again and again wearily, patiently circumventing the obstacles
(casually, or malignantly, or without a thought) laid in its way.
When stunned, though, lying doggo, shocked or asleep,
till the weather turns clement, and the winds drop.

It's not really my business to watch
or analyse this wiggling; only to tend the worm.

But I thought you'd like to know.